The Heritage Collection

The Story of

Champion Sprinter and Dedicated Nurse

Letitia deGraft Okyere

Illustrated by Masum Ahmed

The Story of Rose: Champion Sprinter and Dedicated Nurse
Copyright © 2024 by Letitia deGraft Okyere

Illustrator: Masum Ahmed
Layout designer: Nassim Sarkar

Library of Congress Control Number: 2024916794

All rights reserved.

No part of this publication may be reproduced, stored in a retrieval system, a database, and/or published in any form or by any means, electronic, mechanical, photocopying, recording or otherwise, without the prior written permission of the publisher.

ISBN 978-1-956776-26-3 hardback
ISBN 978-1-956776-27-0 epub

Published by Lion's Historian Press
https://www.lionshistorian.net/

In loving memory of

Opanin Joseph Raddy Kwaku Dede,
Oheneba Madam Christiana Adwoa Nimo,
Charles Ntiamoah Mensah, and Augustus Odartei (AO) Lawson

Acknowledgments

My most heartfelt appreciation goes to Mrs. Rose Amankwaah for allowing me to capture her life's story in this book for children. The hope is that readers will recognize the value of traits such as dedication and commitment and aspire to emulate the example set by Mrs. Rose Amankwaah. I also extend my gratitude to Communications at the London North West University Health NHS Trust for putting me in touch with Mrs. Amankwaah. The publication of this biography for children was made possible through this connection.

> "I've always believed in going the extra mile, and that has served me well during my career. My advice to anyone is to make the right choice and give it 100%.
>
> Rose Asiedua Amankwaah"

Contents

Chapter 1: Dreams of a Little Girl 1
Chapter 2: It's a Girl 3
Chapter 3: Why Rose 5
Chapter 4: Legs Like Springs 7
Chapter 5: Not Just Sweet Talk 9
Chapter 6: More Monikers 11
Chapter 7: Beginning of Change 13
Chapter 8: Inter-Houses Champion 15
Chapter 9: Lady Renault 19
Chapter 10: Spotted by Scouts 21
Chapter 11: Ghana's Sprinter 25
Chapter 12: Final Year at Osei Kyeretwie 27
Chapter 13: Rose Travels to London 29
Chapter 14: The Final Hurrah 33
Chapter 15: Senior Nursing Sister 37
Chapter 16: The Silver Award 39
Epilogue: Looking Forward 43
What Others Said 47
Glossary 49
Fun Fact About Lake Bosumtwe 52
Quiz 53
References 54
Other Books in the Heritage Collection 56

Dreams of a Little Girl

When Rose's mother found out she was pregnant with her ninth child, she hoped for a little girl. Rose's mother, Adwoa Nimo, thought a little girl would even the balance somewhat between sons and daughters in the home. Adwoa Nimo and her husband, Kwaku Dede, Rose's father, already had five sons and three daughters. Yes, Kwaku Dede agreed that, after the last two sons, the youngest son born only three years earlier, a little girl would make a nice change.

For Rose's older siblings, on the other hand, it was not so simple. The boys, led by Charles, wanted a sixth brother, and the girls, cheered on by Beatrice, a fourth sister. Each side made up reasons why the new baby had to be a brother or sister. Each side keenly looked for signs suggesting that the baby would be one or the other. Adwoa Nimo laughed at her children as they peppered her with question after question.

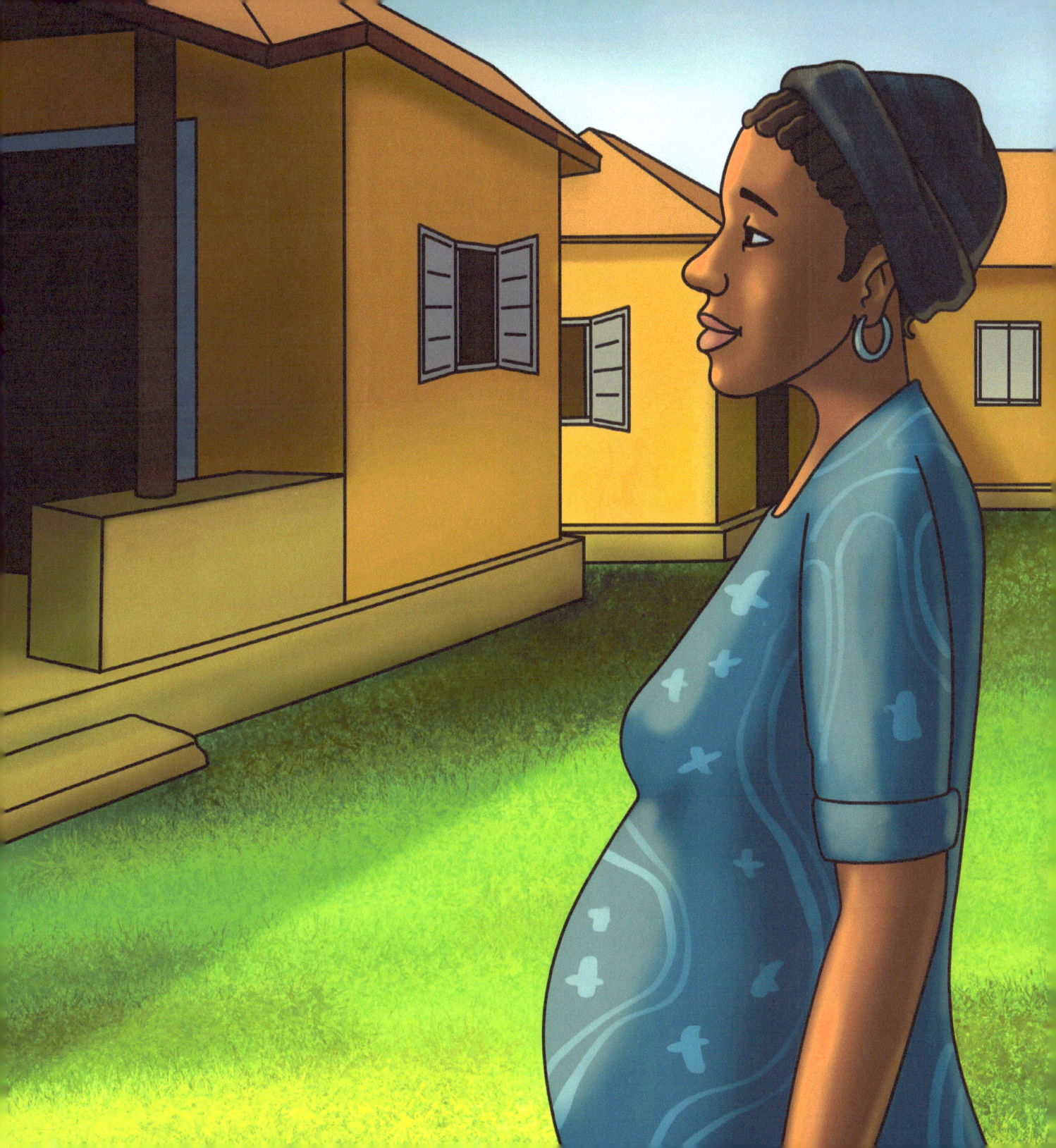

CHAPTER 2

It's a Girl

The family could not wait for Rose's arrival. One warm afternoon in 1952, Adwoa Nimo called out to her husband, "Kwaku Dede, please get me to the hospital." At the time, the older children were at school, and the younger ones were being cared for by Rose's maternal aunt. That evening and night, all the children were restless, eager for Papa, as Kwaku Dede was called by his children, to return home with news of their new sibling.

Rose's father tried to sneak into their Kumasi home through the back door in the early hours of the next morning, but he was caught. Beatrice heard the door click and let the others know, and they all rushed to him, almost knocking him down. After checking if their mother, *Maame*, meaning mother, was fine, Beatrice moved to the next important question. When Papa announced they had a new sister, the siblings burst into song with dance, even the boys. The girls gave them sideways glances. Like Papa, the boys wanted a baby sister, too, but it was more fun to pretend they wanted another brother. "When do we meet our new sister?" they all asked.

Why Rose

Rose's parents had to choose a name for the new baby. Up until then, everyone called her by her *kradin* or soul name. Adwoa Nimo and Kwaku Dede were from Kwahu Aduamoa in Ghana's Eastern Region and, therefore, part of the Akan-speaking people. Akan children acquire soul names based on the day of the week of birth. Rose was born on Monday and went by Adwoa in those early days.

Rose's family set a date for her naming ceremony, called an Outdooring, but Maame rejected every name Papa suggested. None of them felt right. Often, when Maame looked at her contented baby, she thought of roses. Roses come in assorted colors. Roses represent a variety of traits. Roses are a source of joy. Roses have a lasting fragrance. Yes, Maame was convinced; this had to be the name for the baby, who shared her kradin. The Outdooring took place, and Baby Adwoa became Baby Rose.

As Rose grew, the name suited her more, especially pink roses because she was always happy. Baby Rose, as with pink roses, was a symbol of joy and happiness in the home. Maame said Rose smiled and laughed earlier in her development than any of her other siblings.

Legs Like Springs

Rose lived with her family at Bompata in Kumasi, close to the Prempeh Assembly Hall. It was a busy venue for a variety of events, from political rallies to gospel music concerts. Rose climbed up anything she could find to look out of a window, watching the hustle and bustle outside her home. When Rose's nanny placed her down, she just turned around, seeking another ledge to climb.

Sundays were Rose's favorite days. During weekdays, Maame and Papa were traders, keeping long hours at their Kumasi Market shops, while Rose's older siblings were away at school. On Sundays, they all dressed up for worship at the historic Ramseyer Memorial Presbyterian Church in the Kumasi suburb of Adum. When service ended, they stayed for the church picnic at the park or went home for a special Sunday lunch. Either way, Rose could hardly contain her excitement because she loved having everyone around.

When Rose got a little older, she enjoyed running errands around the house. When Papa called, "Rose, fetch my wallet from the bedroom," in a flash, there was Rose with it. It seemed her little legs had springs within. Rose's family teased that she trained for house errands when she ran across the park at the Sunday church picnics. Family members began to use Twi's — the Akan dialect spoken in her home — equivalent of words like "smart," "quick," "swift," and "fast" to describe Rose.

Not Just Sweet Talk

Rose was about five years old when Maame enrolled her at the Adum Presbyterian Primary School, tied to the Ramseyer Memorial Presbyterian Church. Rose enjoyed physical education (PE) because she was the teacher's favorite; it was obvious that she showed promise. She loved that her PE teacher always volunteered her for sporting activities, where she won most of the competitions. As Rose went from grade to grade, though her participation in school sports events increased, it did not dawn on her then that she had a gift. She took her studies seriously as she wanted to make something of her life.

Thus, during school breaks, Rose had no time for friends; she had lots of house chores and helped at her parents' stores. Maame sold African fabrics, and Papa was a wholesale dealer for towels and other household items. When Rose worked at either one of the stores, she assisted customers, completed purchases, and organized stock. Rose hoped to become an administrator or secretary; it would help with managing the stores. So, to Rose, when Maame or Papa fondly referred to her as "Our daughter Rose, the light-footed one," it was just "sweet talk." Her parents were giving her a "big head" before sending her on another long errand. Rose would soon find out that it was not just "sweet talk."

More Monikers

Rose enjoyed learning. After graduating from primary school, she attended St. Cyprian's Anglican for middle school. No surprise there, she became the PE teacher's favorite again and actively participated in sports. Yet still, it had not occurred to Rose that she was a talented athlete. She was focused on a different path. Rose's brother Charles worked at the Standard Bank in Kumasi, and her sister Beatrice was employed at the departmental store UTC (Union Trading Company) in Accra. These just confirmed to Rose that being an administrator or secretary was a useful profession to aim for, she could really make a difference at the shops.

Rose remained unmoved by all the monikers or nicknames from her supposed "swift legs." Even Nana, Rose's maternal grandmother, Adwoa Serwaa, who lived in Kwahu Aduamoa, her hometown, joined the bandwagon. When Rose visited, Nana welcomed her with the appellation, "My granddaughter Rose, the one who is as fast as lightning." Rose's response was always, "Ok, Nana, just tell me what you need me to do. You don't have to fill my head with sweet nothings." To which Nana always replied, "Believe me, child, I know what I'm talking about. Listen to me, my granddaughter." Yet still, Rose did not consider herself a fast runner.

CHAPTER 7

Beginning of Change

Rose passed the Common Entrance Examination and gained admission to Osei Kyeretwie Secondary School (OKESS) in Kumasi. This co-ed boarding institution was the first secondary school in the Ashanti Region, then known as Asante Collegiate. It was renamed Osei Kyeretwie after the private name of Prempeh II, the *Asantehene* or ruler of Asante from 1931-1970. Rose's pending separation from her parents for weeks at a time broke her heart, but she looked on the bright side. First, home was not far away. Second, an older sister, Felicia, taught mathematics at the school. Third, it was a reputable center for learning, and secondary education got her closer to her dream of becoming an administrator or secretary.

In August of 1968, Rose packed her bags for life at boarding school, joining the league of the "King's Children." Students of Osei Kyeretwie are nicknamed *Ahenemma*, i.e., children of a king. Rose was placed in Anokye House with a group of other Form One (or first-year) girls. After her parents got her settled in her dormitory, they turned to leave. Rose bid them goodbye with tears in her eyes, but she quickly wiped them away because she did not want to be mocked by any of the senior students. She was the baby at home, but she was not about to become the baby at boarding school.

CHAPTER 8

Inter-Houses Champion

Rose settled into boarding school life easily. She made new friends, adding to the handful of classmates from St. Cyprian's who had also moved to Osei Kyeretwie. A few weeks after the term (or semester) started, the principal announced the date for the yearly Inter-Houses sports competition. Rose's mates from St. Cyprian's wanted to know if she would participate. Rose thought it was a good idea, and the Anokye House senior prefect helped her register.

Each day after classes, while students went to their dormitories for a rest hour before dinner and evening study time, Rose headed to the sports field to train. She had elected to participate in three events. Most afternoons, there were just a few budding athletes from other houses on the sports field. Rose remained motivated, spending two to three hours daily preparing.

The day of the competition arrived, and the whole school, including staff, made their way to the sports field. Students were dressed in house colors, carrying flags and placards while cheering the athletes in song. Rose's sister, Felicia, had told the family that their very own "Miss Light Foot" had joined the Anokye House team. She would make sure to join her colleagues, taking in every detail to report back to the family.

Rose won all three events she signed up for — 100 meters, 200 meters, and the high jump. The excitement at Anokye House carried on for weeks after the event. Rose became an instant superstar at Osei Kyeretwie, but she did not let it get to her head. However, she began to think that perhaps her family might be right; she did have a talent after all.

CHAPTER 9

Lady Renault

So, even after Inter-Houses ended, Rose continued to train, learning early that it would take dedication to develop her gift. One afternoon after class, the school's senior prefect told her to report to the principal's office. Rose wondered what she could have done wrong. Her days were filled with classes, training, and homework. She did not have time to get into mischief. Why would the principal ask to see her?

Rose walked to the administration block deep in thought. On arrival, the secretary ushered her into the principal's office. Rose was not in trouble at all; the principal asked that she represent Osei Kyeretwie at the upcoming Inter-Colleges games at the Kumasi Sports Stadium. "Rose, we see your dedication. I know you will do well if you represent our great school." Rose nodded in agreement. This was the annual sports competition between secondary schools within a geographic zone.

When Rose stepped on the field for Inter-Colleges, she heard schoolmates scream out, "Rose Asiedua," in song, with pride. Rose participated in four individual events and again came first in all — high jump, long jump, 100 meters, and 200 meters. She was part of the 4x100 meters relay, which Osei Kyeretwie won. When Inter-Colleges ended that year, she was no longer Rose Asiedua, but Lady Renault. Rose's new moniker was taken from the French car company — Renault S.A. — known for motor racing in the early 1900s.

Spotted by Scouts

Rose began to train regularly as a young professional at the Kumasi Sports Stadium when she was in Form Two. One Saturday morning, when training, Mr. AO (Augustus Odartei) Lawson, a sports coach holding keep fit classes at the stadium, offered to be her trainer. AO Lawson was a former sprinter who had represented Ghana (or the Gold Coast as the country was known until 1957) at the 1952 Helsinki Olympics and 1958 Cardiff Commonwealth Games.

In 1970, still in Form Two, Rose participated in the regional competition, on Mr. Lawson's recommendation, representing the Ashanti Region, whose capital city is Kumasi. During this event, Rose was spotted by scouts from what would be renamed the National Sports Council. The scouts went to Mr. Lawson, asking if Rose would represent Ghana in the high jump and 4x100 meters relay events at a friendly game with Côte d'Ivoire. Rose did not win any trophies, and she was disappointed because it was her first assignment outside Ghana. However, Rose did not give up and continued with her training regimen. AO Lawson advised that she was much better suited for 100- and 200-meter sprints, and she gave up the high jump.

For morning sessions, AO Lawson picked Rose up at 5:30 a.m., and she trained until 7:30 a.m. He dropped her back at school, and she prepared for

class. AO Lawson picked Rose up again at 5:30 p.m., training until 7:30 p.m. When Rose returned to school, she took a shower, had dinner, and caught up on classwork. Rose fit her studies around her training schedule. It was hard work, but she enjoyed the fast pace. As Rose trained with AO Lawson, his reputation grew, and he soon had a group of thirty athletes, including Ohene Karikari who would become a champion sprinter.

Ghana's Sprinter

Rose began traveling across the world with the Ghanaian sports team. She went to Kampala for a Ghana versus Uganda competition and to Rome for another international event. In 1972, Rose participated in the "Little Olympics" games held in Germany just before the Munich Olympic Games. As Rose was not competing in any of the Olympic events, Rose attended to her training schedule. She was a little anxious about the upcoming games in Lagos. It would be her first multi-national competition.

In January 1973, Rose was in Lagos, Nigeria, for the 2nd All-Africa Games. Here, Rose would get her big break. Rose won two medals, silver for the 100-meter race and gold for the 4x100 meters relay. Rose's training mate, Ohene Karikari, also won two medals, as did Alice Annum, another member of the Ghanaian team. This was the start of Rose's tag with Alice, when one won gold, the other silver and vice versa.

Rose, now an international champion sprinter, returned to school for what she thought would be quiet months and a gentler training schedule, allowing her to catch up on her studies. However, Rose was selected to represent Africa at the 1973 Afro-Latin American Games in Mexico the coming August. Rose won the gold medal in the women's 200-meter race and acquired another moniker, the "fastest woman in Africa."

Chapter 12

Final Year at Osei Kyeretwie

Rose returned from Mexico to a herald of choruses. Rose's parents and siblings were proud of her achievements. It was exciting for them to flip through newspapers to photographs of Rose on the track, receiving a medal, or taking a victory lap. Likewise, when Rose arrived on campus for what would be her final year at secondary school, she received a heroine's welcome. The boys especially erupted into an uproar, making drums out of anything they could find; Lady Renault had arrived.

She was now in Form Five and would have to prepare for her final examinations, known as Ordinary "O" Level. However, Rose's friends convinced her to participate in the Inter-Houses and Inter-Colleges competitions one last time. Rose's mates got a kick out of watching rivals' hearts sink in defeat just from a sighting of Rose on the field. Months later, she went to Christchurch, New Zealand, in January 1974 to represent Ghana at the Commonwealth Games. Rose won the bronze in the 4x100 meters relay. She now had to buckle down for her O-Level examinations in June.

Rose Travels to London

In August of 1974, a new chapter turned in Rose's life. Her older brother Charles, who had migrated to the U.K. years earlier, invited her to live with him in London to continue with her studies. Rose, not one to remain idle, found her way to the West London Stadium where she trained. Rose enjoyed competitive athletics, but her heart was still set on being an administrator or a secretary, and she discussed this with Charles.

One afternoon, she visited a friend next door and noticed packed bags placed by the front entrance. When she asked, the friend said she was not traveling as Rose thought but was on her way to nursing school. Rose asked how one became a nurse. The friend directed Rose to search the business directory, the Yellow Pages, to identify hospitals with possible openings for trainee nurses. Rose went home to tell Charles she had changed her mind and preferred nursing. After days of checking a copy of the Yellow Pages she found at home, Rose submitted applications to the Central Middlesex, Northwick Park, and High Wycombe hospitals.

Rose got accepted into all three and settled on the Central Middlesex Hospital (CMH) because it was closest to home. A year after moving to the U.K., in 1975, Rose became a student nurse, but she did not give up on athletics. Rose joined the Middlesex Ladies AC, headed by Mrs. Matthews.

She was trained by Zack, the club's coach, and participated in borough and club games. Rose met a young Linford Christie at the stadium and trained with him a few times. He would become a British champion sprinter, breaking the record with twenty-four medals. The West London Stadium would be renamed the Linford Christie Stadium years later.

The Final Hurrah

Rose looked forward to the upcoming 1976 Olympics in Montreal. Rose's superiors at the Central Middlesex Hospital (CMH) encouraged Rose to participate. They put her on work shifts that did not conflict with her training schedule. All her travel plans were made, and Rose was ready to represent Ghana in Montreal. Rose's parents and siblings back home in Kumasi looked forward to reading about her in the newspapers.

About three months before the opening ceremony, Ghana and twenty-one other African nations boycotted the games, protesting New Zealand's participation. New Zealand's rugby team had played in South Africa, a country where there was a policy of racial segregation. Rose was heartbroken; her dream of becoming an Olympian was shattered.

Rose was never one to wallow in defeat, and she continued to train while she turned her focus on her career, opting for theater or surgical nursing. Rose graduated in 1977 and stayed on at CMH, working as a staff nurse in the surgical department. Two years later, Rose was married and looking forward to her first child. When her oldest daughter was born in 1979, Rose stopped training in competitive sports but took a coaching course, allowing her to train budding young sprinters under fifteen years.

Rose would go on to have two more daughters and a son. Rose's three girls and son picked up her love for sports and would accompany her to the stadium to train. The girls showed an interest in gymnastics, so Rose added this sport to her coaching duties. Rose's son became a soccer player. In 1989, Rose returned to club championships at the West London Stadium for her final hurrah, using her married name Amankwaah. Rose did not go home empty-handed; she won the 100-meter sprint and one of her daughters, the Under-11 75-meter sprint.

Senior Nursing Sister

When Rose's athletic career ended, she enrolled at the Thames Valley University to obtain a nursing degree. She graduated in 1993, the same year she was promoted to nursing sister (or senior nurse) for general and minimally invasive surgery. Rose worked with the award-winning Dr. Andrew Menzies-Gow and Dr. Ara Warkes Darzi (now Lord Darzi of Denham) as they developed new techniques and tools in the type of surgeries where smaller cuts are made.

Rose enjoyed being part of the team developing best practices in surgical procedures. These new methods made it possible for patients to return to normal daily activities after surgery faster than before. Rose met many doctors who traveled from all over Europe to her hospital to train under Drs. Menzies-Gow and Warkes Darzi. As a nursing sister, Rose yearned to know more and returned to school, acquiring operating theater, anesthesiology, and managerial certifications. Rose worked with these two internationally recognized doctors for five years before being promoted again.

The Silver Award

In 1999, Rose became the education and theater manager. She was assigned to the Ambulatory Care and Diagnostic Center (ACAD) at the Central Middlesex Hospital (CMH). It was the first of its kind in Europe, marking the new season in healthcare delivery. Prime Minister Tony Blair was invited to open the new center, and Rose took him on a tour, explaining ACAD's equipment and functions. It was an exciting time for the hospital, and Rose was a part of it. Rose managed ACAD's day-to-day activities, ensuring all patients received the approved standard of care.

CMH found that ACAD worked so well they created the Brent Emergency Care and Diagnostic Unit (BECaD) within the ACAD building. BECaD opened in 2006. Rose was present to meet Prince Charles (now King Charles III), who was invited by CMH to cut the ribbon for BECaD during its grand opening. At this time, Rose was a theater matron, managing teams of nurses at CMH's surgical theaters. In 2008, Rose received the ASPIRE Lifetime Achievement Award for her valuable service to the people of North West London. In 2023, the Chief Nursing Officer for England, Dame Ruth May, presented Rose with the Silver Award. This is only given to those who go over and above expectations in their duties. Rose's colleagues had kept it secret, inviting her to a meeting at the last minute.

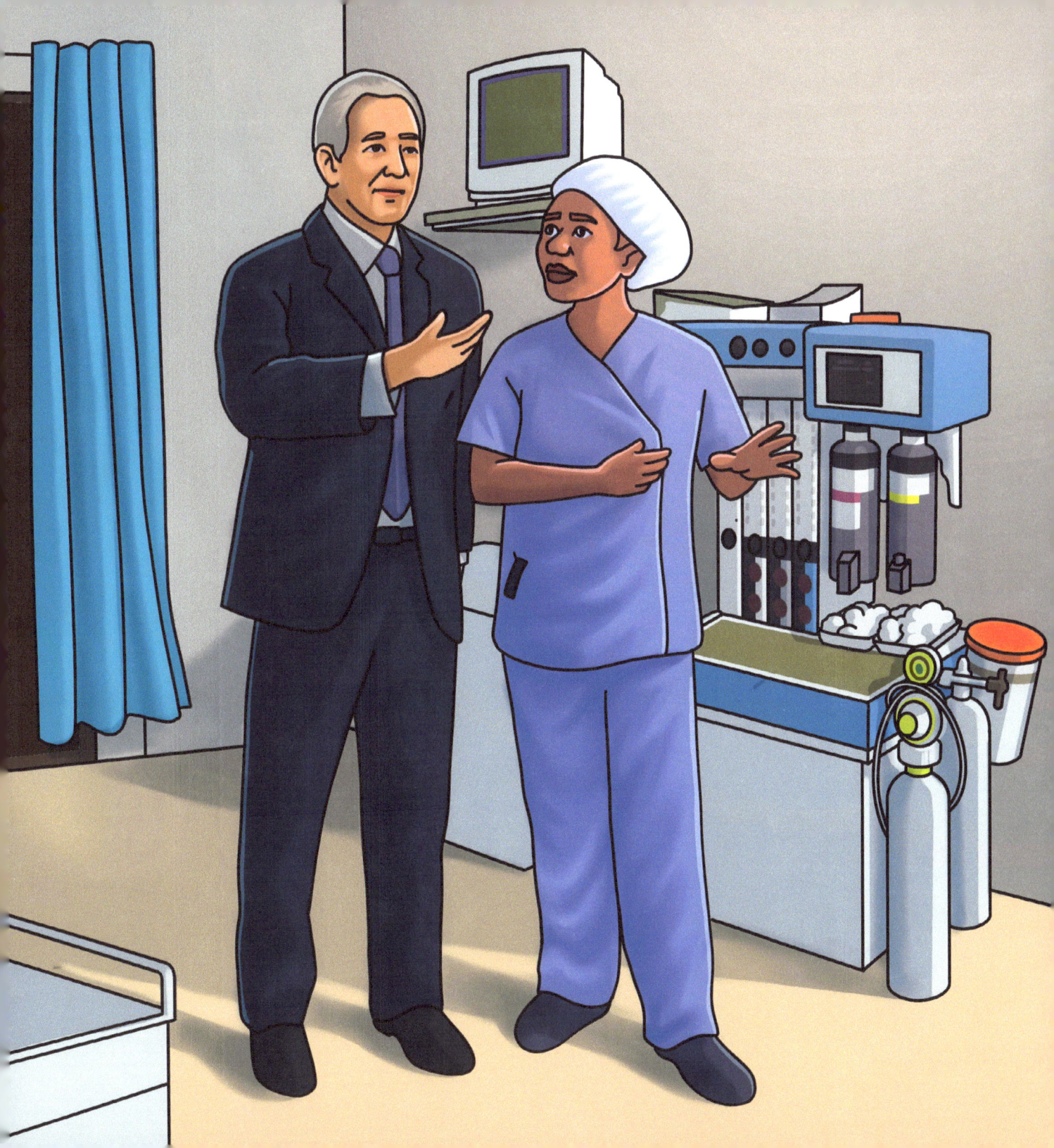

Rose remained a theater matron until her retirement in 2024, after forty-nine years of service. Most of Rose's patients had no idea she was an athletic champion or a nurse with almost half a century of dedicated service. At the time of her retirement, Rose was the longest-serving nurse at CMH. What is Rose's secret? "Always go the extra mile and give every opportunity one hundred percent of effort," she says.

EPILOGUE

Looking Forward

Rose's life has been one of service. When Rose realized that she had a talent, she worked hard, training to represent her region and nation at different national and international sporting events. It did not matter that after many hours spent on the field, she still had schoolwork to complete in the evenings. Rose knew she would need to build a career after athletics. At nursing school, Rose did not stop. She would finish work at 6:00 p.m. and begin training between 7:30 p.m. to 8:00 p.m. Despite several hours at the stadium after a full day at the hospital, Rose would still rise early in the morning for work at the Central Middlesex Hospital (CMH).

In 1977, Rose graduated from nursing school and carried her spirit of dedication to CMH's surgical theaters, giving almost half a century of commitment. Rose worked alongside pioneer surgeons Dr. Andrew Menzies-Gow and Dr. Ara Warkes Darzi. When Rose started at the theater, operations were more open. She was a lead nurse during the shift to keyhole surgery and then to robotic surgery. Whereas patients stayed in the hospital for many days after open surgery, patients could now return home the same day after minimally invasive surgeries. Rose was recognized by Dame Ruth May, the most senior nurse in England, for her years of exemplary service to Britain's National Health Service (NHS).

Now, at retirement, Rose enjoys watching sporting events with her family in real time. She was glued to the TV during the 2024 Paris Olympics. She spends her time encouraging younger generations to believe in themselves and to work hard towards their goals. Rose knows firsthand that once you embark on a course of action, you must remain committed to doing the best possible.

It has not been all quiet for Rose. On October 14, 2024, she was at the Queen Elizabeth II Center in Westminster, London, for the NHS Parliamentary Awards. She received the prestigious Lifetime Achievement Award for building a legacy in healthcare. Rose was nominated by Bob Blackman, a U.K. Member of Parliament. In his nomination, he wrote, "She was instrumental in developing a multi-skilled theater workforce with a strong emphasis on self-development." Rose had an enjoyable evening, mixing with all the other nominees and award winners.

The life of Rose Asiedua, now Rose Amankwaah, is a lesson on the value of excellence and dedication in one's chosen pursuits. Worthwhile traits that open doors beyond one's imagination, such that a little girl from Bompata in Kumasi would grow to train alongside sporting champions in Ghana and across the world like Linford Christie, work with legends in the surgical field, meet world leaders, and give forty-nine years of devoted service, earning the NHS Silver Award and NHS Parliamentary Award.

What Others Said

It's fantastic to work under her; she always has a positive attitude. She's always passing on her experience to other colleagues; she never keeps things to herself. Anyone who comes under her will go up and up and learn. She's like a mum to everyone. We're really privileged to work under her.

Jayantha John, CMH colleague
Nishat Ladha (BBC Sport Africa), March 19, 2024

Throughout your career, you have exemplified what it means to be a matron. Your nurturing spirit, strong leadership, and unwavering dedication have touched the lives of countless patients, their families, and your colleagues. You have been a source of comfort and strength during difficult times and have consistently gone above and beyond to ensure the best possible care for those in need. Thank you from the bottom of our hearts for your selfless service and unwavering commitment. Your contributions have made a significant difference and will continue to have a positive impact on the lives of many.

CMH colleagues
CMH Retirement Brochure for Rose Amankwaah, March 28, 2024

Glossary

Ashanti Region	Ghana is divided into regions for administrative purposes. Ashanti Region is in the southern part of the country.
Asantehene	The king of the Asante people in Ghana is known as the Asantehene. Asante (Akan Twi language) is also written as Ashanti (English language).
Kumasi	This is the capital city of the Ashanti Region and Asante Kingdom in Ghana. The Asantehene is also the ruler of Kumasi, i.e., Kumasihene.
Common Entrance Examination	Until education reforms in the late 1980s, students' admission to secondary or technical school was based on the Common Entrance Examination (CE) score. The CE, a standardized test, was generally taken after six years of primary school education.
Ohene Karikari	A Ghanaian sprinter who represented Ghana at the 1972 Munich Olympics. He won two gold medals (100- and 200-meter sprints) at the 2nd All-Africa Games held in Lagos, Nigeria, in 1973.

Nursing sister	A female nurse, usually of a high rank or grade.
Hospital theaters	Rooms in hospitals where surgical operations are carried out.
UTC	Union Trading Company was a Swiss trading company connected to the Basel Mission. It had business interests in Ghana, Nigeria, and India.
Twi	Twi is a dialect of the Akan language spoken in south-central Ghana.
Prempeh Assembly Hall	A multi-purpose event center for government and private functions located in Kumasi.
Osei Kyeretwie (OKESS)	The first secondary school in the Ashanti Region of Ghana, then known as Asante Collegiate. It was renamed Osei Kyeretwie, after the private name of Nana Prempeh II, Asantehene, from 1931-1970.
Inter-Houses	Competitive games between houses (dormitories) at a school.

Inter-Colleges	Competitive games between secondary schools within a zone in a Region.
Central Middlesex Hospital	It is located on the border between the London boroughs of Brent and Ealing. It was first created as a health care center for the poor in 1903, going through several extensions to become the Central Middlesex County Hospital in 1930.
Minimal Invasive Surgery	This is when surgeons operate using a method causing less damage to the body. In general, this type of surgery results in shorter hospital stays, less pain, and fewer complications.
ACAD	The Ambulatory Care and Diagnostic Center at the Central Middlesex Hospital. It was the first of its kind in Europe.
BECaD	Brent Emergency Care and Diagnostic Centre at the Central Middlesex Hospital provides critical care in emergency cases and high-specialization consultations.

Fun Fact About Lake Bosumtwe

Lake Bosumtwe (or Lake Bosomtwe) lies sixteen miles from Kumasi. About 1.07 million years ago, a stone meteorite created a crater 1,150 feet deep and it filled up with water, becoming the largest natural lake in West Africa. Lake Bosumtwe is fed by rain because there are no inlets and outlets. A local legend tells that in the seventeenth century, a hunter spotted an antelope (*otwe* in Twi) and chased after it. The antelope jumped into a small pool of water collected in the center of the crater. The hunter waited for days, but the antelope never came out. The shocked hunter named the area Bosomtwe meaning god of the antelope, because he believed the water had saved the antelope.

Quiz

1. Which secondary school did Rose attend?
    a) Adum Presbyterian School
    b) St. Cyprian's School
    c) Ramseyer Memorial School
    d) Osei Kyeretwie

2. How many siblings did Rose have?
    a) 8
    b) 4
    c) 7
    d) 9

3. At which games did Rose win her first gold medal?
    a) Ghana versus Côte d'Ivoire
    b) 2nd All-Africa Games
    c) Ghana versus Uganda
    d) Munich Little Olympics

4. Where did Rose train as a nurse?
    a) Northwick Park Hospital
    b) Barnet Hospital
    c) Central Middlesex Hospital
    d) High Wycombe Hospital

Quiz Answers: DABC

References

Amankwaah, Rose. "Some Additional Clarification." Received by Letitia deGraft Okyere, 14 May 2024.

Amankwaah, Rose. "Rose Amankwaah Manuscript." Received by Letitia deGraft Okyere, 25 April 2024.

Willis, Anna. "North London nurse who's been at same hospital for 48 years has a secret - she was once 'fastest woman in Africa.'" *My London News*, 9 April 2024, https://www.mylondon.news/news/real-life/north-london-nurse-whos-been-27904093. Accessed 25 April 2024.

Amankwaah, Rose. Personal interview. 10 April 2024.

Ladha, Nishat. "Rose Amankwaah: The London nurse who was an African sprint champion." *BBC Sport Africa*, 19 March 2024, https://www.bbc.com/sport/africa/67456164. Accessed 9 April 2024.

"'Fastest woman in Africa' retires after 50 years in NHS." *BBC*, 12 March 2024, https://www.bbc.com/news/uk-england-london-68518301?fbclid=IwAR2u0UPo0Vu1wAB5p02wv04YvLYMZkBBOb0VEcipbQJmQ89Q9yGNetI9I-Uo. Accessed 9 April 2024.

Amankwaah, Rose. Personal interview. 19 March 2024.

Mitchell, Chris. "Former international sprinter from Harrow announces retirement after 50 years with NHS." *Harrow Online*, 5 March 2024, https://harrowonline.org/2024/03/05/former-international-sprinter-from-harrow-announces-retirement-after-50-years-with-nhs/. Accessed 10 March 2024.

Ford, Steve. "Hospital archives turn up nurse link to royalty and running." *Nursing Times*, 25 May 2018, https://www.nursingtimes.net/news/hospital/hospital-archives-turn-up-nurse-link-to-royalty-and-running-25-05-2018/. Accessed 10 March 2024.

Other Books in the Heritage Collection

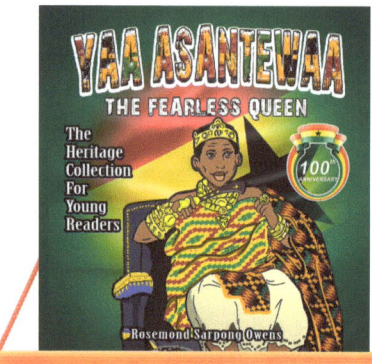
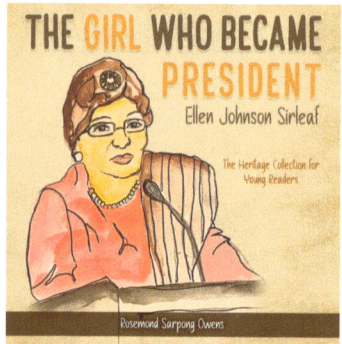
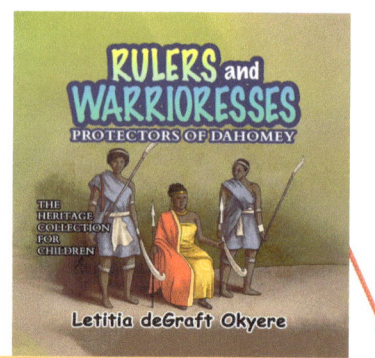
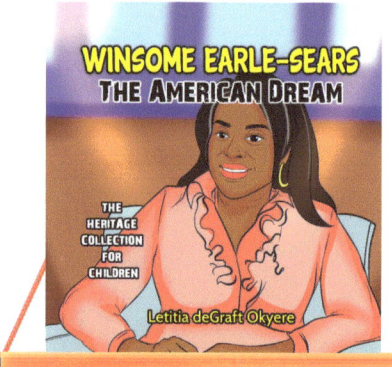
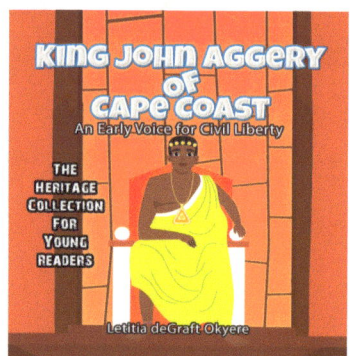

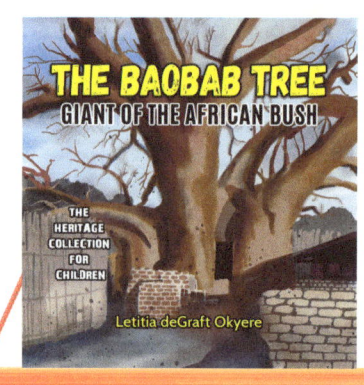
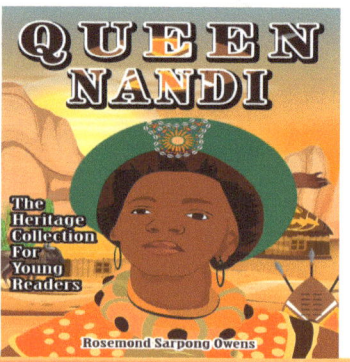
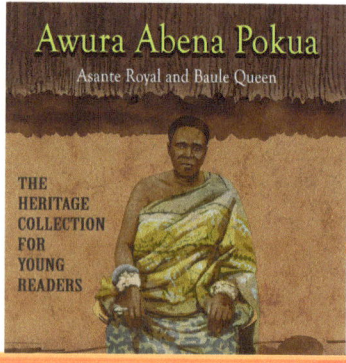

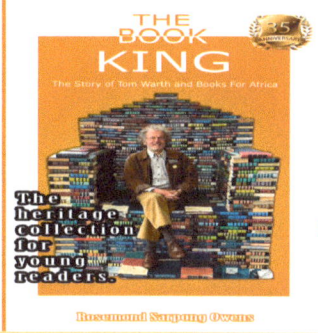
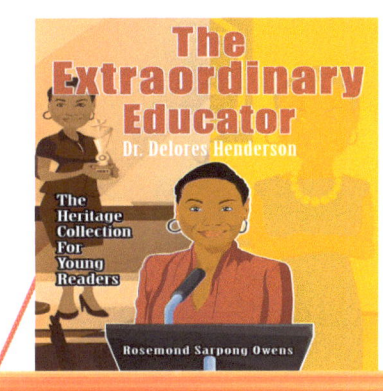
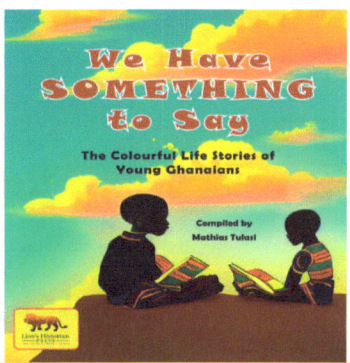

> "There is always going to be someone better than you but that shouldn't stop you from trying your best. You must be your own champion and give 100%."
>
> Rose Asiedua Amankwaah

www.ingramcontent.com/pod-product-compliance
Lightning Source LLC
Chambersburg PA
CBHW041407010526
44107CB00015B/1104